ANGELO FRONTONI

MOVIE STAR PORTRAITS
THE NAKED CELEBRITIES

Introduced by
ALBERTO LATTUADA

To Ursula Andress as a tribute to her overwhelming
mythical beauty and in recognition of a working
partnership that has lasted thirty years, during which time
she has steadfastly refused to pose for other
photographers. Thank you, Ursula.

ISBN 88-7301-001-6
Copyright © 1990 by Gremese International s.r.l., Rome
English translation copyright © 1991 by
Gremese International s.r.l., Rome
Casella postale 14335
00149 Rome

Translation of I miei nudi celebri
Translated by Shula Curto
Edited by P.E. Fogarty
Jacket design by Silvia Notargiacomo
Phototypeset by Grafica Internazionale, Rome
Photolithography by Studio Bondani, Rome
Printed and bound by Conti Tipocolor, Calenzano
(Florence)

English titles of foreign language films are given when the
film is commonly known by that title.
In the other cases original foreign titles are given with
English literal translation.

Cover photograph: Florence Guérin

Grateful thanks to all those directors — among whom Lamberto Bava,
Mauro Bolognini, Alberto Lattuada, Gianfranco Mingozzi, Antonio Pietrangeli,
Peppino Patroni Griffi and Franco Zeffirelli — without whose friendly assistance
many of the photographs in this book could never have been taken.
A special thank you to actress Florence Guérin,
who kindly agreed to pose for the jacket.

PREFACE

by Alberto Lattuada

*The Bible says: In the beginning God created the heaven and the earth
and then the seas. He created living creatures and plants to populate and
embellish these three kingdoms and Eden became a place of great beauty.
But God understood that the earth needed cultivating in order to flourish
and an audacious idea took shape in his mind: with the dust of the earth
he made man in his own image. He breathed into his nostrils the breath
of life and the man became a living soul. But he was alone.
And now we come to the most mysterious part of the Bible story. The
Lord God caused the man to sleep, and whilst he was asleep took one of
his ribs and from it created woman. He left them, naked and
"unashamed", to roam at will through the Garden of Eden. But God
gave a warning: "Eat freely of the fruit of all the trees, but do not touch
that of the tree in the midst of the garden". We all know what happened.
The serpent tempted Eve, who ate the apple which she then offered to
Adam. It was fruit from the tree which reveals the knowledge of Good
and Evil. Adam and Eve knew that they were naked and sewed fig leaves
together to cover themselves. Awareness of Good and Evil means total
awareness of life itself, while the question of free will, born of
transgression, poses problems that are virtually unsolvable.
Incidentally, have you ever wondered why the male of the human species
has breasts but no milk to offer? This trace of bisexuality, an erogenous
zone for males too, gives rise to all manner of speculation. Was it
perhaps an oversight on the part of the Lord? And why is man so
attracted to woman? As though driven by an unconscious desire to
reestablish his original status, that is to say before the famous rib was
removed.
The Book of Genesis offers no clue.
With Angelo Frontoni we are back in Eden. His creations have yet to eat
the apple (or fig, according to some critics) and are therefore naked.
As a token of the age-old "sin" of nakedness, several of Frontoni's
models have chosen to present the spectator with two round, finely-
sculptured, innocent-looking hemispheres.
Yet a moment later we realise that the very nakedness of the female body
possessing these gifts combined with a certain facial expression hints at
far deeper secrets. For example: the features of Jane Birkin insinuate
both childlike innocence and an abyss of guiltless perdition.
Going back to our two hemispheres, or in less poetical terms the buttocks
or arse, surely the most eloquent examples are those of actress Daniela
Poggi, who, back to the observer, provocatively contemplates the view
from the window! Nadia Cassini's pose is reminiscent of Modigliani*

(whose exhibition of some very frank nudes in Paris in 1918 was closed for indecency on the first day!); and, in fact, Frontoni has skillfully created an elongated effect, expressed in a single sinuous line running the entire length of the body, so characteristic of this Italian painter's later works. There is just a hint of a small, neat breast and her lips are slightly parted as though she had intended to speak but changed her mind.

Each face in Angelo Frontoni's book seems to express a different sentiment, and we are instinctively led to consider not only the aesthetic value of the nude figure before us, but also the innermost nature of the model herself. For three or four thousand years painting and sculpture alike have sought to express the divine beauty of the naked human body. But twentieth century man seems bent on repudiating his origins, on destroying this model of perfection, to the extent that today's nude is all too frequently a tattered, ugly shadow of its former self, and the face it offers, devoid of inner life. Cinema and television delight in this ferocity, and the critics offer little or no opposition. The violence of a satanic Adam explodes on the screen masquerading as a form of art. I have my doubts as to the aesthetic value of such an operation.

But we were talking about Angelo Frontoni and the pure and chaste provocation of his photographs. Obviously, I cannot discuss his entire repertoire in this brief introduction. But here are a few of the thoughts that spring to mind as I explore the pages of this gallery. At a glance, Ornella Muti's gentle eyes have a magnetism that seems to draw the observer inexorably into a secret understanding. The desire awakened by the sultry features of Monica Guerritore is made all the more acute by the challenge of an obstacle in the form of a black veil exploding upwards from between her thighs.

Eleonora Giorgi hides her head in the sand, almost as though she were

Alberto Lattuada and Nastassia Kinski on the film set for *Stay as You Are*

ashamed of the latent vitality hidden in her supple body.
The alabaster incandescence of Patty Pravo's almost androgynous figure is accentuated by the girl's eyes.
No point in trying to understand the secret of Ursula Andress, for it is in this very enigma that seems to envelop her whole being that her charisma lies.
For the first time we can discern innocence in the naked figure of an actress, Milena Vukotic, and the total confession of her innermost sentiments.
The strength emanating from Fabio Testi's powerful torso seems to flow into Charlotte Rampling's upthrust arms, moulding them into a cosmic embrace.
On the last page Elena Sofia Ricci casts us a calm, indulgent yet penetrating glance. The shadow of a shadow of an unformed smile bears witness to a fact we all recognise; that a young girl has become a woman, Eve perhaps...
Peruse, explore, decipher the profound significance of each of Angelo Frontoni's portraits.
Photography is more complex than cinema, which can deceive the eye with movement and sound. Photography is tantamount to theft: a brief moment in which the man behind the camera astutely extracts a mute confession from his victim.

9

Alberto Lattuada
Dalila Di Lazzaro
and Angelo Frontoni.
Rome, 1988.

MY FAMOUS NUDES

by Angelo Frontoni

My famous nudes.
"Why famous?", one might ask. It is simply that many of the pictures in this book were a personal scoop of mine, in as much as the protagonists agreed to pose in the nude for me and me alone: for the first and, often, only time.
From Sylva Koscina, who, in 1960, was the first actress in Italy to be photographed in the nude, to Elena Sofia Ricci, 1990, this volume is a rare collection of unforgettable moments, emotions, images and memories. I hope it is as special for my readers as it is for me.
A heartfelt thank you to all my actress-models.
A special thank you to Ursula Andress and Ornella Muti, Alessandra Mussolini and Patty Pravo, the Kessler twins and Anita Ekberg.
And, finally, my very special gratitude to Ira Fürstenberg, who agreed to the publication of photographs, which she helped me choose, that have never been seen in print before.
My love to you all.

Angelo Frontoni

CONTENTS

SYLVA KOSCINA

Rome 1960. The first Italian actress
to be photographed in the nude.

15

Rome, 1974.

URSULA ANDRESS

Rome, 1976. On the set of
E.G. Castellari's film *Scaramouche.*

Rome, 1974.

Zambesi river, Zambia, 1975.
On the set of *Africa Express* .

LAURA ANTONELLI

Rome, 1972. Screen-test for
Salvatore Samperi's *Malizia* (Malice).

Rome, 1984. On the Film
Set of *La Gabbia* (The Cage),
by Giuseppe Patroni Griffi.
With Toni Musante.

JANE BIRKIN

Rome, 1976. For Giorgio Capitani's film
Bruciati da cocente passione (Burned by a Scorching Passion).

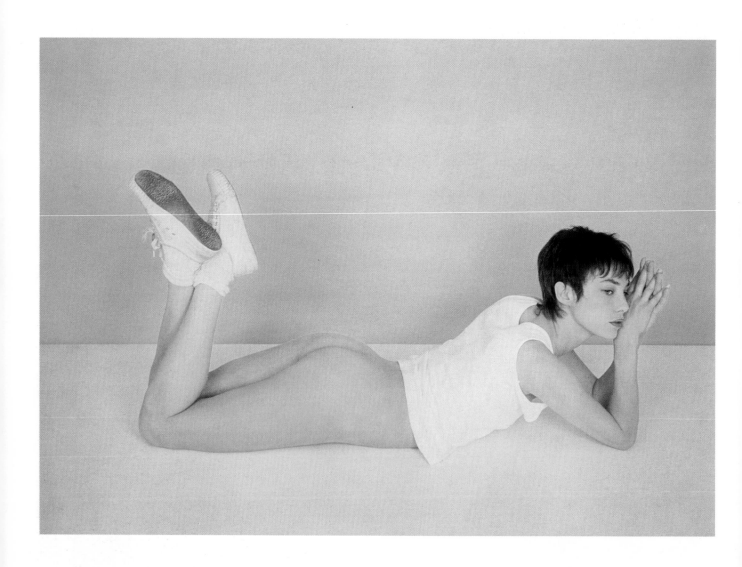

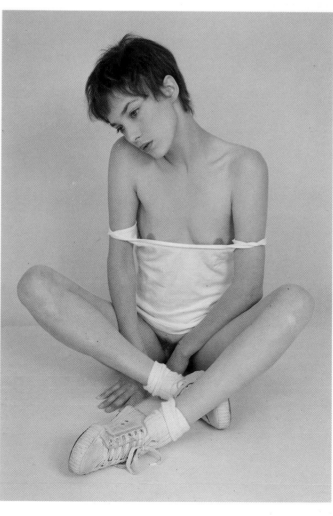

CARROL BAKER

Trinidad, 1974.

32

NATHALIE DELON

Rome, 1970. On the film set of
Le sorelle (The Sisters), by Roberto Malenotti.

BARBARA BOUCHET

Rome, 1975. On the film set of
Mauro Bolognini's *Down the Ancient Stairs*.

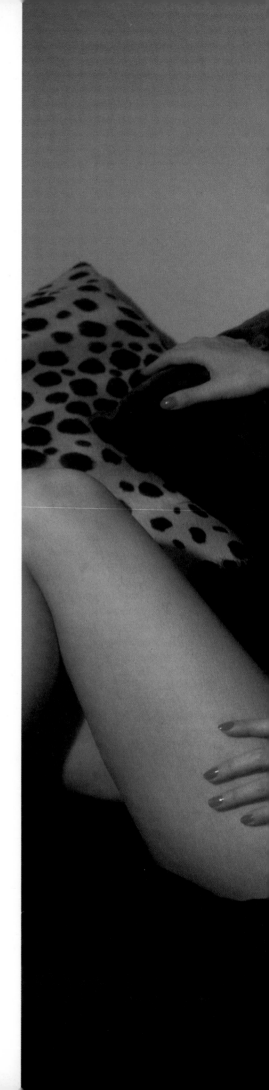

ANTONELLA LUALDI

Rome, 1978.

ANITA EKBERG

Rome, 1984.

ELSA MARTINELLI

Rome, 1976. On the film set of Luigi
Faccini's *Garofano Rosso* (Red Carnation).

BARBARA BACH

Sardinia, 1979. On the set of Sergio Martino's
film *L'isola degli uomini pesci*
(The Island of the Fishmen).

MARIA ROSARIA OMAGGIO

Madrid, 1976. On the film set for Vincente Escriva's
La lozana andalusa (The Andalusian Lozenge). Opposite page, Rome, 1980.

PATTY PRAVO

Rome, 1975.

CHARLOTTE RAMPLING

Sabbioneta (Mantova), 1971. With Fabio Testi on
the set of Giuseppe Patroni Griffi's film
Addio fratello crudele (Goodbye Cruel Brother).

CORINNE CLERY

Almeria, Spain, 1981. For Willy S. Regan's film
The Last Harem.

Rome, 1986.

73

FLORINDA BOLKAN

Brazil, 1978.

76

ELEONORA GIORGI

Rome, 1978.

ORNELLA MUTI

Malibù, Los Angeles, USA, 1980.

AGOSTINA BELLI

Rome, 1976. For Dino Risi's film
Telefoni bianchi (White Telephones).

MARIANGELA MELATO

Rome, 1984.

NASTASSIA KINSKI

Madrid, 1978. On the film set for Alberto
Lattuada's *Stay as You Are* with Marcello Mastroianni.

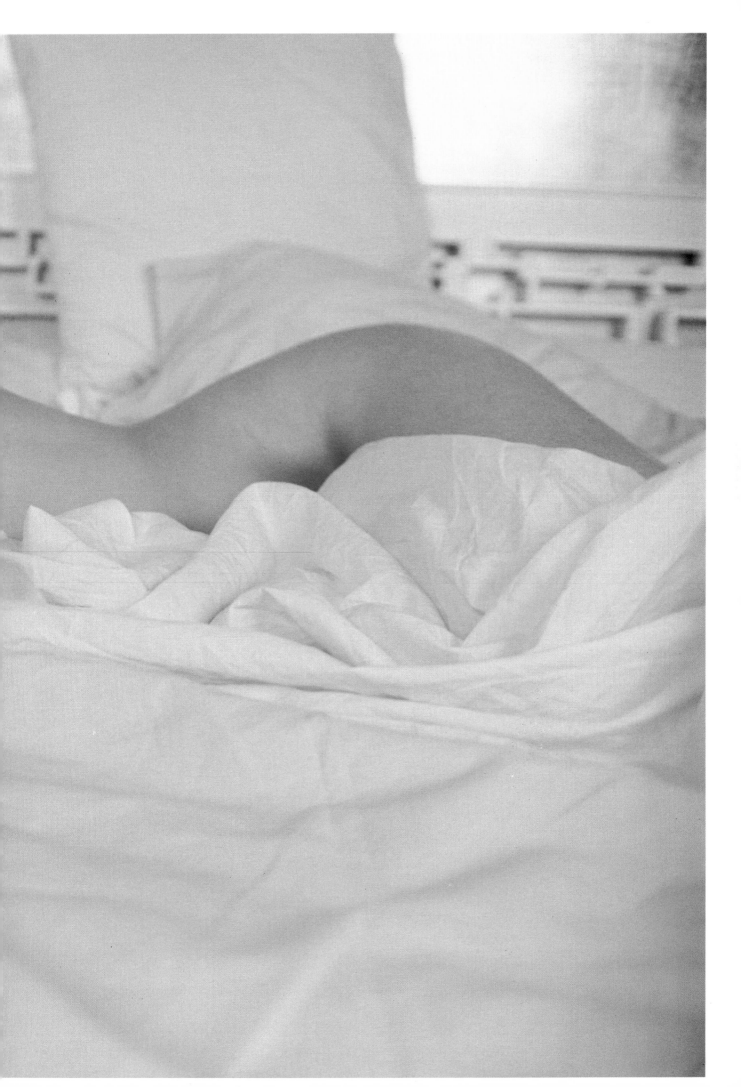

BARBARA DE ROSSI

Rome, 1989. On the set for Ludovico Gasperini's
film for television *Oggi ho vinto anch'io*
(Today I Won, Too).

ORNELLA VANONI

For the 1978 photo reportage *L'uomo oggetto...*
(Man as an Object).

MONICA GUERRITORE

Rome, 1987.

AMANDA LEAR

South west France, 1983.

MARISA MELL

On the set of Lucio Fulci's 1969 film
Una sull'altra (One After the Other).
Opposite page, Rome, 1980.
On the following
pages, with Helmut Berger
for Sergio Grieco's film *Belva con il mitra*
(Beast with a Machine Gun).

ELKE SOMMER

On the 1970 film set for Jean Negulesco's
The Invincible Six.

SERENA GRANDI

Paris, 1984. On the set of
Gianfranco Mingozzi's film
Le avventure di un giovane Don Giovanni
(The Adventures of a Young Don Giovanni).

Right, Rome, 1987. On the set of
Lamberto Bava's film *Le foto di Gioia*
(Photos of Joy).
Following pages, Rome, 1985,
on the set of Tinto Brass's film *Miranda*.

ZEUDI ARAYA

On the film set of Sergio Corbucci's *Robinson
Crusoe* 1977. Opposite, Trinidad, 1974,
on the set for Luigi Scattini's film *Il corpo* (The Body).

DANIELA POGGI

On the set of Biagio Proietti's film *Sound*, 1988.
Below, with Peter Fonda.

ELEONORA VALLONE

Malindi, Kenya, 1980.

ALESSANDRA MUSSOLINI

Rome, 1987. For a screen-test.

IRA FÜRSTENBERG

Rome, 1970. For a screen-test for Franco Zeffirelli's
Brother Sun Sister Moon.

DALILA DI LAZZARO

Rome, 1978.

ALICE and ELLEN KESSLER

Rome, 1978.

ISABELLA FERRARI

Rome, 1985.

DANIELE GAUBERT

Sardinia, 1969. On the set of Antonio Pietrangeli's film
Come, quando, perché (How, When, Why).

NADIA CASSINI

Rome, 1975. Following pages, Rome, 1983.

SYBILL DANNING

Rome, 1975.

TINA AUMONT

Rome, 1970.

ROSSELLA FALK

Rome, 1972. During a performance of Diego Fabbri's
play *La bugiarda* (The Liar).

151

MILENA VUKOTIC

Rome, 1975. With the cooperation of
Alessandro Blasetti.

DELIA BOCCARDO

Rome, 1978.

MARIANGELA D'ABBRACCIO

Rome, 1989. For the theatrical
production *Dannunziana*
(The Dannunzian Woman).

ELENA SOFIA RICCI

Rome, 1990.

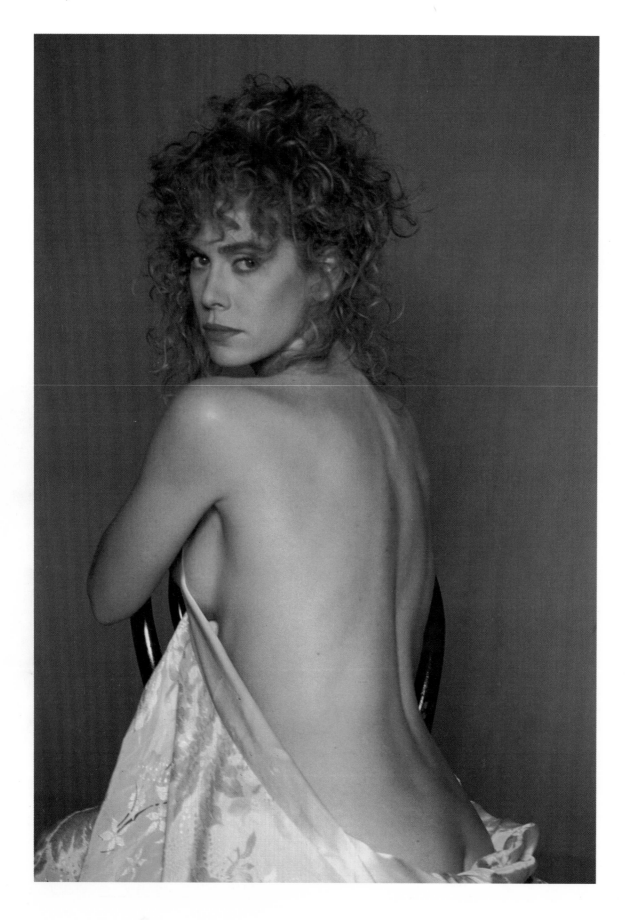